ADAH

Rejected, Betrayed, Healed!

Dionna Dibble

Scripture taken from the King James Version of the Bible.

WestBow Press books may be ordered through booksellers or by contacting:

WestBow Press
A Division of Thomas Nelson & Zondervan
1663 Liberty Drive
Bloomington, IN 47403
www.westbowpress.com
1 (866) 928-1240

ISBN: 978-1-4908-4055-0 (sc)
ISBN: 978-1-4908-4056-7 (hc)
ISBN: 978-1-4908-4054-3 (e)

Library of Congress Control Number: 2014910559

Printed in the United States of America.

WestBow Press rev. date: 10/14/2014

Contents

Epigraph

I call her Adah. She's the nameless woman from Scripture who met Jesus at the well, and hers is a story that details the pain of rejection and the deep scars of betrayal, as well as the miraculous healing and deliverance from the hopelessness of a life tortured with bitterness and unforgivenss.

Preface and Acknowledgements

There was a chill in the evening air, so we grabbed sweaters and took our Bible class of young adult girls out to my back patio. We pulled our chairs up near the warm glow of the fire-pit, and I began weaving a story. It was the story of the woman Jesus met at the well. I began to draw word pictures, and the girls seemed captivated. As I drew from my childhood experiences of growing up in a third-world culture, I imagined a girl called Adah, a girl who had not been able to choose love for herself but had been forced into one failed marriage after another.

Adah had only known one relationship of complete, unconditional acceptance from a man, and that man had been her father. But Adah's father changed, and her life spiraled from one painful disappointment to another until she found herself destitute, her life and soul poisoned with bitterness beyond recognition. What would become of her? Would there ever be hope? Adah thought not, but wait… Who was this stranger who was telling her all the things she had ever done?

As this fireside story began developing, I found myself adding to it for weeks and months, and friends began encouraging me to write it in book form. Then along came Peggy Readout, my friend, encourager, and Christian mentor, who helped tremendously. Thank you for your sweet generosity, advice, perspective, and keen eye! I will always cherish your godly example!

Thank you to Deedra Linder for the many hours of editing. Collin Pace, Christine Andro and MaryBeth Dibble, this project would not have been the same without your help.

I also want to thank my parents, Robert and Belinda Filkins, who obeyed the call of God and took my sisters and me wherever He led. The education-by-exposure I received throughout my young life gave me a greater cultural perspective than if I had only lived in the familiarity of our great home nation, the United States of America.

To my children, Blake, Kara, Travis, and Justin, thanks for being the best kiddos in the world! The writing of this tumultuous story immersed me in psychological trauma that our family is otherwise unfamiliar with, and I thank you for your understanding. I won't forget all the extra chores you did around the house when I was so consumed with the story that I needed your help. I'm so thankful that the doctor who told me I'd never bear children was wrong!

A million "thanks" would never be enough for the love and support of my husband, Tom. You have given me the security to grow personally and allowed me to be myself, even when that person was exasperating to live with. For twenty-four years now, you've led me lovingly and challenged me to grow in my relationship with God. Your love and example of faithfulness and loyalty will always be a treasure to me!

Last, but not least, thank You, Jesus, for allowing me to know You. I can't even breathe without Your help! You are my hope, my life, my salvation, my healer, my strength; You restore my soul… well… You're my everything!

Chapter 1

Adah

Humming cheerfully to herself, Adah sighed heavily but contentedly as she walked along the pathway with her mother, Dina, and her sister, Maya. They strolled slowly toward the house as the day came to an end. The sun sat in the western sky with a magnificent display of brilliant colors, and a cool breeze ruffled the wisps of hair that had wriggled their way loose from her head covering. It had been a glorious day indeed!

Father often said Adah was meant to be a goat child because she skipped and hopped everywhere she went. "Adah's girlish skipping and romping throughout the day has loosened all but her perfectly white teeth."

"Why should she walk when she can skip?" Adah's mother playfully defended. "When there's joy in your heart, shouldn't it also be in your step?"

Adah was the last of ten children - eight sons and then two daughters - and she had a most happy childhood. For years her father, Harmon, unlike many of their neighbors, had been a God-fearing man. He trusted in the prophecies that Jehovah would come as the Messiah and make things right. He followed the traditions of his Jewish roots and kept the laws of Moses. He brought his family up with a secure teaching of hope and a firm hand of loving leadership. His sons had grown up and become strong leaders of their own families and were well respected in the community as their father had been in earlier days.

Harmon had followed all the teachings of the forefathers, performing their annual sacrifices and keeping all the feasts. Oh, the feasts were Adah's favorite times! There was food and laughter. There was the time of recounting the stories of old, reciting the law, and explaining the sacred traditions of the feasts that gave these celebrations such significance. There was singing and dancing in a circle with the other ladies and girls while the men and boys sang along and clapped their hands. Then Adah would sit with her chest heaving under heavy breaths and sing, clap, and watch as the men and boys gathered in a circle to take their turn dancing. The celebrating was fantastic, and Adah loved it most of all because her big brothers would bring their wives and children, and they would all be together. Some of Adah's nephews and nieces were her age and some were older, but they were all very close. She knew each of her brothers adored her and her parents cared so deeply for her.

So it was with sheer pleasure that Adah's tired legs carried her home that evening, her basket swinging carelessly by her side. Just that morning that same basket had carried melt-in-your-mouth loaves of bread made from her mother's own recipe, the recipe she shared only with her daughters. The family had gathered by the threshing floor of Harmon's field to dress their dinner. They feasted on the kid Father had been feeding well. Josiah, Adah's youngest brother, had provided the firewood. Only the finest from Mother's vegetable garden was what Maya had brought. There were also the honey wafers from Adah's oldest brother's wife and many other delicious things. It had been a wonderful feast indeed!

Harmon's family had observed the feast in private as the rest of their community continued on with their normal daily routines. It had been many generations since any of them had followed those particular feasts because these people had long since been rejected by the Jews and felt no loyalty to Jewish traditions. For you see, Moses had instructed the Jews long ago in the book of the law called Deuteronomy that they were not to intermarry with the Gentiles. They were to keep their race pure because the Promised One would come through the loins of this people. So when their Jewish fathers took wives of the unconverted Gentiles, they were now a mixed breed of Jew and Gentile, causing the full-blooded Jews to despise them. All their families had been ostracized and put out of the Jewish camp. They eventually settled here in Samaria and had long since remained a separate and shunned people. For many generations it had been this way, but Adah's father had been different.

Being brought up in a community of people who were ostracized and shunned by the servants of Jehovah had not dampened the flames of loyalty and hope in Harmon's heart and neither had it silenced his voice of leadership as he taught his family the ways of Jehovah. He was determined to bring his family up properly, the way any son of Abraham should - the way his father had taught him.

However, recently the harshness of six consecutive years of crop failure, health problems, heartaches, and hardships had overshadowed Harmon's hope in the Messiah. He had allowed it to dull his devotion to Jehovah, embitter his spirit, and dampen his celebration of life.

The bitterness over losing Caleb, his third son, and then losing his wealth finally had changed him, and he was no longer the kind, gentle man Dina had married some forty-seven years earlier. All he seemed to care about was regaining his wealth and erasing the shame of poverty from his reputation. This caused him to be a bit harsh with his family at times. He had become somewhat disgruntled, keeping the feasts only out of a sense of duty so as to not disappoint his family. Dina worked hard to keep a cheerful atmosphere in their home, and Harmon attempted to camouflage his cross demeanor most of the time, but nothing escaped Adah's sharp eye and inquisitive nature, and she wondered often about it all. Just today, Adah had noticed Father simply going through the motions and not really enjoying the feast, the singing, and the dancing the way he used to. The spark was gone from his eye, and the spring was missing from his step.

"Is Father losing his faith in Jehovah?" she worried. "Is he going to become like the other fathers of Samaria?" To Adah, it seemed the other fathers led their families on and on in some endless quest for wealth that amounted to nothing more than crops, herds, and property being passed on from one generation to the next with no meaning whatsoever. She didn't want to imagine her life being like that of other girls in her community. Her mouth went dry, and she shook her head to clear her thoughts.

These questions lurked in the back of Adah's mind, but she put them far from her as often as she could to hold on to her happy childhood days as long as possible. Some of the other girls were anxious to grow up and become women - to have a husband and children to care for - but Adah was content to be her mother's little girl, her brothers' little sister, and the apple of her father's eye.

She *was* the apple of Harmon's eye, and she knew it. "A beautiful child," Adah often heard people say of her. Yes, she was smart and hardworking like Maya, her sister who was three years older, but Adah was also pretty. Her smart black eyes sparkled as they watched everything around. Maya used to say Adah had a perfectly shaped nose and that her eyebrows perched in perfect arches over her eyes. Harmon always said that his favorite of all Adah's physical attributes was her gleaming smile. "When I come through the door, your perfect teeth light up the room more than a freshly cleaned oil lantern," he used to say. So in spite of her growing concerns and apprehensions about life, Adah smiled often.

Chapter 2

Growing Up

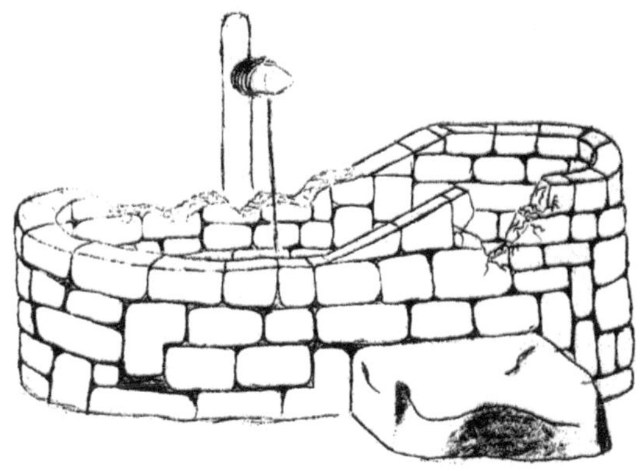

Adah was almost fifteen when she finally became a woman. Many of the other girls had made their fathers proud by coming into their womanhood earlier, and Adah's mother had begun to grow concerned about her. Maya had started her flow of womanhood by the end of her twelfth year, and her mother had started hers when she was thirteen. The common worry of that day was that if a young girl did not come into womanhood at the expected time of life, then she might be barren and bring shame to the whole family.

So Dina was greatly relieved as she sat there that day and explained to her youngest daughter that this bleeding she was experiencing was a normal part of life now and she would become accustomed to it. Regardless of what her mother said, however, Adah didn't feel relieved at all. This was not fun!

But Harmon was only too happy! That same day, he talked to all the men at the marketplace and near the gates about it and about their sons. He was hoping one of the wealthier men would choose Adah for his boy to marry. This way, he could get a larger bride price for her than he had negotiated for Maya.

Even though Maya was not so pretty, she was a hard worker and a good cook, and she had only been married eleven months when her first baby was born. And to top it off, it was a *boy* she had borne to the young husband who bought her. The whole family was proud of Maya, and there was much discussion about her firstborn being male. Little Levi was almost four now, and he had two younger sisters. Both families were very pleased with Maya.

By the third time Adah had her womanly flow, she had figured out that, for her, it always came with much cramping, backaches, and terrible headaches. The very idea that this was to be a normal part of her life was something Adah did *not* want to get used to!

Her mother had explained to her the process by which she would someday bring a baby into the world, and now that she was experiencing such great discomfort already with her womanhood, she wasn't looking forward to marriage at all. It wasn't that she would mind the cooking and housekeeping. Adah, like her mother and sister, was a very good cook. Her mother had trained her well, and she was not afraid of work, but she had heard Maya describe pregnancy and the delivery of her babies, and the idea of all those changes happening to *her* made Adah feel quite disconcerted.

Nevertheless, her father returned from the market one day on top of the world.

"Come and let us celebrate, for our family has been honored again, and I will soon be rich!" Harmon cried as he entered the door. Dina stopped her work and dipped Harmon a drink of cool water.

She brought it to him as he sat down, "Oh, Harmon, you *are* shrewd! Who have you made a deal with this time? He *is* a good boy, isn't he? He will treat my baby girl well?"

Feigning hurt feelings, Harmon cocked his head sideways and pulled away from Dina. "Of course, he's a good boy! His father is the wealthiest in the region, and the bride price he has offered for Adah is even more than I paid for you!" he teased.

Chapter 3

Hassan ben Ruben

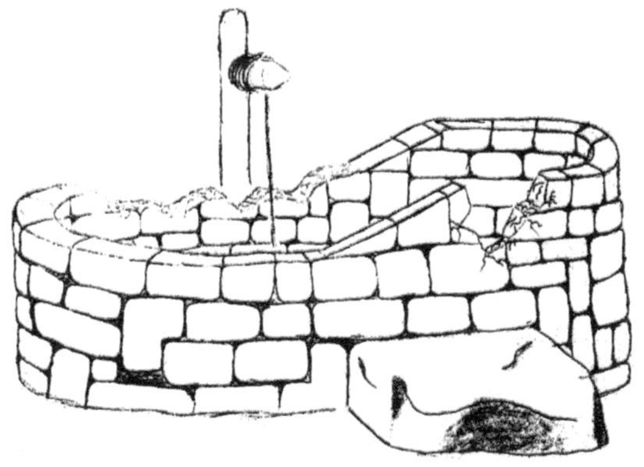

And so, within the year, at age sixteen, two years older than her sister had been, Adah was married and became the wife of Hassan ben Ruben.

Hassan was a decent fellow. He had been well trained and was nice to look at, but due to his father's wealth, the servants had indulged almost every wish, and Adah was his new servant. She worked hard to keep his house clean and tidy. She planted a wonderful garden and was an excellent cook. Hassan was quite pleased with the meals she prepared and was enthralled with her beauty, but when he took her to bed at night, she experienced unspeakable pain every time and found it hard to respond to him gratefully.

Adah continued to be the best housekeeper and cook she could possibly be. "Soon," she said to herself, "this will get easier the way Mother said it would, and Hassan and I will make a happy home and family the way my parents did."

Hassan was enchanted and mesmerized with the beauty of his young wife and somewhat intrigued that this peasant girl with lean, strong muscles and the most beautiful smile he had ever seen actually belonged to him to do with as he pleased. Adah had picked up her mother's habit of humming while she worked, and Hassan would often stand around the corner when Adah didn't know he was there, just to listen. She hummed the joyful songs that her family was accustomed to singing at feast times. She hummed the soothing melodies Mother sang to her as a young girl at bedtime. She hummed songs that she made up as she went along. Adah loved to hum, and Hassan loved hearing it. "She is happy to belong to me," he told himself. This idea that he had a happy wife gave Hassan confidence that he was a good husband and that he would someday become a good father of many children and gain much respect in his community by leading a happy family.

But time went on and Adah's pain did not go away. She tried to explain to Hassan how she hurt, but he pouted and was offended that she didn't find him delightful. After a few months, he began to strike her in exasperation when she winced or pulled away from him.

"You stupid woman, can't you give me the bare basics of life?" he raged.

Things didn't get better the way her mother told her they would, and eventually, after only eleven months of marriage,

Hassan put Adah in a cart and took her back to Harmon. Right in the public market, Hassan demanded the immediate return of Adah's bride price.

Adah was horrified and humiliated! She would now be considered a disgrace to her whole family. How would she ever be able to face her brothers and their wives at the next feast? In addition to the fact that the whole village would find out about her shame, Harmon had already spent some of the money. So now, in order to pay the Ruben family back, he made a deal to give them the mule that pulled his plow. He would have to barter or borrow from neighbors from now on to even prepare his fields, and the whole matter would cast him in a poor light within the community. While he was groveling and making this embarrassing deal in the market place, Adah slipped away and ran home, not bothering to go inside.

Harmon stomped up the walk calling Adah gruffly away from her mother's garden where she had hidden herself, pulling weeds and watering the herbs with bitter tears. He was furious about the whole situation and stressed from the unfavorable deal he had been forced to make with Hassan ben Ruben.

He dragged Adah by the arm as she half-walked, half-ran to keep up with his angry pace. As he shoved her through the door ahead of himself, he hissed through clenched teeth, "Adah, you useless girl!" The grip he had on her arm felt like it would leave a bruise, and she fell weeping to the floor in front of her mother.

"Harmon! What has happened?" Dina cried as the commotion brought her away from her mending and to her feet. She quickly searched Adah's face then Harmon's angry expression. What could possibly have taken place, and why was Adah here without Hassan?

Harmon curtly informed her that Hassan had rejected Adah because she hadn't pleased him. He then proclaimed his exasperation at the loss of money and the mule, as well as at the public humiliation he had faced. He kept on until Adah was crumpled on the floor, sobbing. He hadn't once shown any concern for what Adah may have been feeling.

Dina used her most soothing voice as she attempted to calm her husband, "Now Harmon, we haven't even heard Adah's side of the story yet. Maybe there's an explanation. Come here, honey, tell Mother what has been going on."

"Well then," Harmon said disgustedly, throwing his hands in the air. "I'll leave you two at it. Maybe your silly woman talk and a good cry will do this girl some good and fix her. I'm going to have to let Ruben calm down for a few days, and then maybe I can work something out with him. You'd better teach her what the duties of a woman are! She'd better be good for *something* after all the trouble she's put us through."

Even more painful than Adah's injured pride was her broken heart. She felt hurt and rejected by Hassan, yet what hurt most deeply were the words and actions of this new, strange person who used to be her loving father. He had adored and protected her, but now he seemed to despise her right along with Hassan ben Ruben. Where was the father who had cherished her for who she was? Who was this man who valued her only for what he could gain from her? Adah felt the pain of betrayal added to the sting of rejection. She wondered where all the tears could be coming from. Her heart, soul, and mouth felt so dry and parched that she thought she wouldn't even be able to swallow much less produce more tears, but they kept coming as her mother cried right along with her.

A week went by, and Harmon finally spoke to elder Ruben at the market place, but young Hassan had already asked his father for a different girl, and the negotiations had already begun. The whole Ruben family was disgusted and displeased with Harmon and his daughter Adah. Even though Harmon had hoped Adah's beauty and hard-working manner would make up for the fact that she did not come from a wealthy family, Ruben and his son didn't see it that way. They figured they should have known better than to take a chance on this ungrateful peasant girl who was not even willing to do her main duty as a wife, and Hassan wanted nothing more to do with her.

Ashamed and humiliated by the conversation that had been overheard by several people near the gate, Harmon gave up for the day and went home to pull the plow himself. Through clenched teeth he muttered, "I will just work off my anger and try to figure out what to do about this disgraceful situation tomorrow."

Later that evening, after Harmon had cleaned his plow and put it away, he walked wearily down the path to the edge of the small river. "A swim will do me good after working like an animal all afternoon," he thought to himself.

As he passed the neighboring farm, Samuel came out and walked beside him. Samuel had been Harmon's neighbor for many years, and the same drought that had put Harmon's crops in jeopardy six years in a row had affected Samuel's wealth in the same way. They both had suffered loss, not only of wealth but also of status in the community. They understood one another, and Harmon was grateful that Samuel, even though he had no doubt heard about the current situation with Adah, chose not to mention it.

They walked in silence, and, like a good friend, Samuel waited for Harmon to bring up the topic of his humiliation from Adah.

When Harmon finally mentioned it, Samuel had a proposal. Since his family had also been through rough times, Samuel had no bride price money set aside with which his son Zephniah could buy the wife of his choosing. Zephniah was the age to be married, and Samuel thought that if he let Harmon use his mule to pull the plow, maybe Harmon would let Zephniah take Adah in exchange. This way both families would benefit.

Even though Harmon had hoped to get some financial profit from Adah, the idea of having the use of Samuel's mule was tempting at this moment. His muscles ached with every weary step. Besides, Harmon was also relieved to imagine himself letting the other men at the market place know that his beautiful, young Adah had been desired and claimed again so soon. So they shook hands and made the deal.

Chapter 4

Zephniah

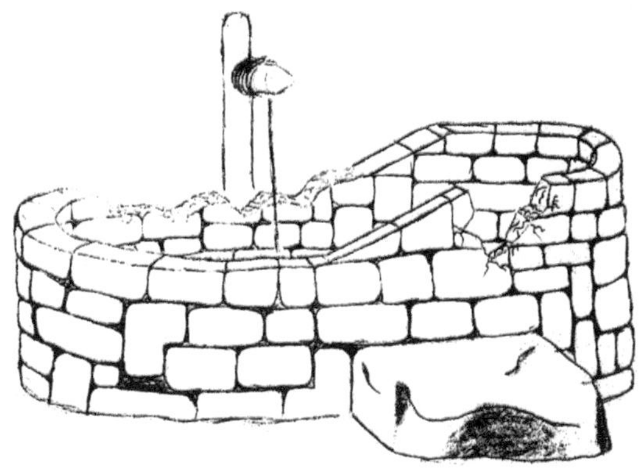

Later that year, Adah was married again - this time to Zephniah. It felt awkward and strange. He was the boy next door, and not only was he her brothers' friend who used to tell her to get lost and leave them alone, he was also the one who had called her the daughter of a poor man and never apologized when his father fell to the same lot. Adah had not forgotten his cruelty, and her mouth went dry at the very sight of him.

He was a bit arrogant with no obvious reason, and Adah had never liked him much. But now she was to belong to him. The idea made her feel queasy inside, but this marriage was the least she could do to erase the shame she had brought upon her father.

The marriage between Adah and Zephniah was not like the one she had with Hassan, it was worse. Hassan had almost pitied her at first because she came from such a poor family. He had at least appreciated her cooking and tidy house, and he was quite vocal in his comments about her beauty.

Zephniah, on the other hand, already looked down on her for being poor although he was no better off. She knew he had hoped for someone else. In fact, Adah had an idea which girl Zephniah had longed for, but since his father couldn't afford her, Adah had been the only option. He treated her with disdain even though she did all she could to pretend to enjoy meeting his every need.

As time passed, however, the intimacy ritual of the evenings became easier for Adah. The pain was not so great anymore, and whatever her problem had been seemed to be going away. So she did everything she could, day and night, to please Zephniah, and by the sixth month of their marriage, she missed her womanly flow.

Soon, a little bump in her abdomen was the indication of new life growing inside her, and Adah felt more happiness than she had ever known before. All her fears about the physical process of birth that haunted her previously disappeared at the thought of having her own little baby to love and care for. Both families were proud, and even Zephniah seemed semi-pleased with his wife. He began dreaming of the things he would teach his son.

Maybe this is what the good life was supposed to be like. Happy memories from Adah's childhood were beginning to emerge from the dark fog that had shrouded them for the past few years. She began making plans of her own about how she would raise a family and make a happy home the way her mother had done. She would not think of her seething bitterness over the changes in her father. Maybe the recent past would become like a distant nightmare and Adah would be able to forget her shame as she immersed herself in blissful motherhood.

"I will forget Hassan and the way he rejected me," she told herself. "I will forget the way Zephniah used to be. I will be happy from this time on."

There was much to keep them busy, and Zephniah continued to grow fond of the idea of having his own little family. When he returned from the fields, he would wash up and then fondle Adah's little bump and talk to the baby. Adah began using her smile again, and Zephniah smiled back and even acknowledged her beauty a time or two. It was almost like these two had been strangers, and now they were beginning to get to know each other and embark on the mystical process of maybe even falling in love. He helped her prepare their small, humble home for the arrival of this joyous occasion, the birth of their first child.

Early one morning, Adah hummed a tune to herself as she carried the bucket of water from the well to do her morning washing and other chores. Suddenly, she felt a twinge of pain from her abdomen. She put the bucket down for a moment until the pain subsided and continued on with her day's work. By noon, however, she had started to bleed and cramp; and within three terrifying days, her bleeding ended and her little bump was gone, taking with it the joy in her heart, the smile from her face, and the admiration in her husband's eyes.

Zephniah seemed to revert back to his old self immediately. He resented Adah for losing the baby and began treating her harshly. She tried to conceive again but developed an infection from trying too soon after the miscarriage. As fever racked her body, Zephniah called her lazy for lying around instead of doing her chores.

How could he be so insensitive? How could he not see that her heart was broken and *her* hopes were shattered too? How could he think only of his own disappointment and grief?

The roots of bitterness in Adah's heart, although buried deep down, immediately began to sprout and grow vines of hatred again. They grew up in her spirit, twisting around all her thoughts and choking out everything good that was left. Her hatred was not only for Zephniah; it was also for Hassan Ben Ruben, for her father, and for the cruel blows life seemed to deal her one right after the other. She longed to be a little girl again with only her chores, her play, and the love of her mother. She longed to live in her little world of fantasies that things were going to get better some day, but experience had taught her that bitterness was her only reliable friend, and so she held tightly to it. Attempts at keeping a cheerful disposition like her mother's had failed her, and Adah felt herself embracing the dull depression and bitterness that seemed to have gripped her father for almost a decade. Adah's soul seemed to be drying up like the barren fields during the long, unyielding drought when rains did not fall.

Adah became more and more bitter until she would actually speak back harsh words to Zephniah, and he often slapped her for it. Most women of that time and of that culture thought nothing of being slapped by their husband when he was angry, but Adah had been brought up differently, and she was not accustomed to that type of harsh treatment. She refused to cower but instead defiantly stared back at Zephniah, letting her bitterness ooze through her stony glare; then she would turn her back disrespectfully on him and walk away while he was still talking to her. She allowed her actions to tell the story of how much she resented him. He had never been nice to her when they were growing up, and the romance they had while she was expecting their baby had been short lived. She had not one shred of gratefulness or loyalty toward Zephniah.

Adah knew it wasn't right, the way she acted, but she was so enveloped in the dark fog of her grief and bitterness she could not bring herself to care about right or wrong. She just knew that *she* had been wronged and was living in a defensive mode, justifying her actions in her own mind. Time went on and the more she justified herself, the more emboldened she became and the more brazenly she displayed contempt for her husband. Soon, Adah found herself speaking out disrespectful retorts to Zephniah regularly and berating him with her words.

Then the day came that Zephniah took her back to Harmon to break the deal his father had made, while Adah stared blankly at her father's feet. She knew only too well how disappointed and angry he would be. They had been here before. She knew, and it hurt her to know, how much aggravation she was to him. So she hardened and braced herself against his fury and the cruel lashing he would no doubt give her.

But after Zephniah had his say and left, Harmon did not shout the way Adah had anticipated. Instead, he hung his head, took her gently by the arm, and led her into the house to her mother. Her parents were both aging quite visibly now, and even Dina seemed to have lost some of the passion for life that had once kept a spark in the atmosphere of their home. There was no more laughter, no more teasing, not even any yelling.

The three of them sat down and stared at the floor, and Harmon sighed heavily. "Well, Girl, go get the water and help your mother with the work. You may as well at least make yourself useful around here."

Adah knew it was too much to hope that her father would offer some kind of comfort. He had long since replaced the type of fatherhood that would have tried to bring some reassurance to his daughter with one of indifference to her feelings and needs. Did he not see how hard she had tried? Had he no feelings left for her at all? Had all those sentiments of love they shared in Adah's younger years been artificial, or did he really have the ability to abandon them and brush her aching heart aside like some pesky annoyance? Adah decided that maybe he wasn't worth her time either.

Long, dreary days turned into longer, wearisome weeks, and several months passed. Finally, at the end of one long, uneventful Sabbath, Harmon sat down and told his wife and daughter to do the same. "I've done a great deal of considering of late," he said flatly, "and I've come to a conclusion."

Dina and Adah both stared at him, wondering what light he could possibly shed on their bleak situation.

"I've done a major part of Samuel's work to pay for the use of his mule, and the crops we yield this harvest should sell for enough to pay him off completely and help us move," he said.

"Samuel sold last year's crop for enough to buy my land. If his mule was sufficient to plow both his field and mine this past season, then his mule can plow them both when I sell to him. That's what we'll do. We'll sell this farm and move away from Sychar to another part of Decapolis - a region called Galilee, north of here. It will be a new place where we can start over. We won't tell the people of that region we're Samaritans. We'll speak only Hebrew and follow their traditions and no one will have to know any different."

Adah's heart jolted forward at the thought of a new place - a place where no one knew of her shame, where no one looked away when she came near, where conversations didn't curiously pause when she walked by. She hoped this would work, yet she knew how difficult this would be for her parents. They had put everything into this farm, and so many years of hard work along with their hopes and dreams had been born and lost here.

"But Father, shouldn't this land go to Adin, the eldest son? Isn't there something in the Law of Moses about it being a curse to sell your land? I have brought so much ill on this family!" Adah buried her face and sobbed quietly.

"No, my daughter, do not weep," Harmon soothed. "I was fooling myself all those years to think it would benefit me to follow Moses' law. This land is not even the true heritage of our Jewish fathers. That went to the sons of their Jewish wives, not to us. I have done this family a great disservice to imply we were as good as Jews. We are really nothing more than the other Samaritans around here and the poorest of them, at that! We've spent way too many years on wasted traditions. I have no more reason to stay here. We will surely leave this place. It will be best for you and for me. All I've gained here is a scar on the good name I passed on to your brothers. They have fared better than I, and it will benefit them if I am gone and the memory of their father is erased from the land. We can pass for Jews in Galilee if we keep to ourselves. It will be best."

Harmon seemed decided, and Dina didn't object. If this really were a chance for her daughter to find someone who would love and cherish her, then she was on board! Dina had so lovingly cared for her children and trained her daughters. She knew Adah, her youngest, had a good work ethic, a gentle nature, and a beauty any man could love if the circumstances were right.

So they made the deal with Samuel, packed their belongings, paid the traveling fare to a man with two camels, and made the move. Their new village was far enough away that no one knew anything about them, but it was still close enough to travel back and visit the extended family once a year.

Chapter 5

Shefar'im

Adah loved the small farm in Galilee her father purchased with his earnings from Samuel. It was situated just on the outer edge of a small community called Shefar'im, convenient to the marketplace yet off the beaten path and away from the stares of curious onlookers. Adah knew it was completely natural for the villagers to wonder about her small family - being strangers, newcomers, and all - but she had been through some difficult ordeals and did not wish to make any of their acquaintances.

So when the afternoons wore on and the work was all done, Adah would go sit in the grass on the west side of the house. She would watch the sun set over the rolling hills that spread as far as the eyes could see. The property had a small stream that gurgled happily near enough to the house that she could hear it after a heavy rain. The sound of it made Adah feel as if she would never have to feel that dried up feeling again. Those days of torment with Zephniah were such dry and bitter days for her soul. But then she would shake her head and decide not to think of Zephniah or the tiny soul that would have been her baby or any of those sad and mournful times anymore.

The new property also had a barn just large enough for a hay wagon, a few of Father's tools, and some grain storage. Adah loved the barn on rainy days. She would go there, sit among the bags of grain, and think positive thoughts by contemplating how grateful she was to her parents for being willing to give up so much for her.

"But then again," Adah consoled herself, "this move seemed to be a benefit to Father as well. This farm is small and more manageable for him in his later years." She was not yet ready to completely forgive him for the first two marriages he had arranged for her, and allowing herself to be grateful to him seemed too close to forgiveness. Adah was not ready for such a step as forgiveness toward her father, so she held tightly to the idea that Harmon's primary motives for coming here were probably selfish and not for her benefit in the least.

Sometimes, Adah would fancy herself to be a real Jewish girl who trusted in Messiah. Living here among God's chosen people gave her hope, if only in her daydreams.

Although she spent most of the day helping her mother in the house or vegetable garden, Adah would steal away to the barn to be alone with her thoughts and the smell of grain as often as she could, especially when the day was wearing on. There was a reason for this. In years past, the evening was Adah's favorite time of the day because Mother would gather the children around so Father could instruct them and share with them his values and thoughts of the day. Leaving the house at this time of the day and going out to watch the sunset or sit in the barn was Adah's way of showing disdain to her father but in a deniable fashion.

She resented that he hadn't continued to be the same man he had been when she was small. "Why did he have to get so bitter? Why did he have to let down on the teachings that held our family so close together? The drought had not forced him to change; he allowed it to change him!" Adah judged him. She wondered if Father's illnesses and Caleb's death had been a curse for his bitterness over losing his wealth. Then she shook her head again, trying to dismiss all the negative speculations.

All the while, Adah never noticed she was harboring the same bitterness that had ruined her father. She didn't realize it was eating away at her soul. She still saw herself as being gentle and loving like her mother, eager to find the good in others. She was convinced this place was allowing her to heal from her recent past and that she would once again be a tender-hearted young lady her father could love again.

"Oops, there I go again trying to adjust myself and become eligible for my father's acceptance. When am I ever going to learn that the problem is with him? He's the one who has let poison come into his soul. I will dismiss thoughts of him, thoughts of Hassan, thoughts of Zephniah. I will cleanse myself of those negative meditations and be free from the darkness!" Adah got up, went to the stream, cupped her hands, and drank deeply, trying to erase the confusion from her mind. Then she went into the house to help Mother finish the evening chores and display her cold indifference toward her father.

Although Adah had lived here in this pretty place less than a year, it was a significant time to her. She convinced herself that she had made progress as she searched her inner self for answers and melted into the solitude. She went to the brook often for a drink of fresh water and believed she was cleansing the negative identity from her soul to make herself new and happy again.

Each day, Adah would go to the stream an extra time and, even though the pot at the house was still more than half full, would carry another full bucket of cool water back and let the overflow slosh over drenching her legs and feet. Then she would envision the refreshing feeling coursing through her spirit and making her strong. Adah felt certain this was a new beginning for her.

Chapter 6

Melkhana the Wheat Farmer

As Harmon began to establish himself in the new community, he encountered a man in his thirties who, after mourning the death of his wife, was beginning to become interested in finding another. This man specified that he was mostly looking for a woman who could keep house and cook. Harmon believed this would be a good opportunity for Adah. Surely, she could cook and clean as well as, if not better than, this man's former wife, and this would cast her in a favorable light. So Harmon made the deal.

Melkhana gave Harmon a young mule, and Adah was married again. She was very apprehensive going into this marriage and quite understandably so. She had already been married to two men who had failed to love her for who she was, and this man had made it clear he was not looking for someone to love, only for someone who would work. However, Harmon had made the deal, and so the marriage was arranged and done.

Melkhana was an easy-going man and didn't expect much. He was pleased with Adah's housekeeping and cooking and complemented her generously. His first wife had been barren, so he had known disappointment in life too. He was cheerful and pleasant, and Adah felt within the first few weeks of marriage to Melkhana that she would be able to forget all her disappointments and finally be free to make a happy home, have happy children, and live a happy life - the way Mother had done.

Adah and Melkhana became soul mates, and for the first time in her life, Adah had someone with whom she could share her true feelings. They lay awake late into the night sometimes out on the hay wagon and talked about... well, everything. Melkhana told her all about his childhood and his first marriage. He told her the hopes and dreams of fatherhood that had been shattered upon the realization of his wife's barren condition and of his lack of money to buy another wife. "Besides," he said, "I loved her completely and didn't really desire another, until I met you, that is..."

"Had that been why Melkhana's specifications for a wife had been limited to the housekeeping aspects?" Adah wondered. "Was it because he didn't think his heart could ever love again?" There was a long, pensive silence between them as they gazed up at the stars, not thinking about the stars at all. Eventually, Melkhana broke the silence.

"What about you? Tell me about your life."

Adah told Melkhana all about her happy childhood, her brothers, her sister, and the many happy feasts, and she told him the long, sad story of her two marriages and losses. She was sure to throw in enough details of their Jewish traditions to make it seem as if they had, indeed, been upstanding Jews all along and not simply Samaritans who held to some Jewish beliefs. She lied and told Melkhana they had come from Tel Adashim. She remembered passing through there on their journey here. When Father had stopped at the market to purchase some bread and gather information on the area, she had taken a walk around the village and acquainted herself with it somewhat. It was a larger village, and Adah figured Melkhana would not know enough about it to ever question more than she could handle.

There was a hint of guilt that tugged at her conscience as she told these lies to the only man she had ever really loved, but Adah did not want to risk him finding out she was a Samaritan and ruin her chance at happiness. Besides, she was not sure she believed in Jehovah anymore anyway. She figured that God hadn't seemed to be able to make her life turn out very well so far, so why should she be concerned with following His laws? She would just have to make her life what she could make of it on her own. Maybe Father was right about all the wasted traditions. "I will trust no one besides Melkhana and myself," Adah told herself. That was how she would live out the rest of her days, seeking her own happiness and the happiness of Melkhana. "That will make a happy home," she concluded, content with her reasoning.

Silence fell between them again as they lay there on the wagon, each of them lost in thought. The story of Adah's two lost marriages had touched Melkhana deeply, and he was sad for her.

"You are so tender and beautiful!" he told her. "I don't know how you came through such terrible happenings and still manage to be so pure and tender."

Adah let herself try to believe she was indeed pure and tender. She allowed tears to fall as the sadness of her story washed over her again. She denied the hardness that was deep inside her causing her to bear up under the lies she had just told. She knew she would have to be ever on her guard to keep the story the way she had told it that night. Her husband must never know the full truth about her.

Melkhana held her close as she cried and tried to keep the truth and the lies all straight in her mind. They were all mixing together, and she felt so overwhelmed, but Adah told herself that the tears would wash her heart clean. Then Melkhana made tender love to her under the stars, and Adah knew she would soon conceive and bare a child to this man she adored. She was finally sure this was how life was supposed to be!

When planting time came, Melkhana and Adah worked hard together putting their seed in the ground. They were not only preparing for crops, they were building a life together - one that would be rich with love and secure with the respect they had for one another.

They settled into a comfortable routine, and Adah enjoyed keeping house and cooking her delicious recipes for Melkhana. Mother had taught her the proper use of so many herbs and spices from the garden, and Adah had become a master at it.

When they were in the fields, Melkhana always made Adah stop working before he did so as to have a bit of rest time before she would need to begin preparing the meal. "I don't want to work my beautiful treasure till she's all worn and tired," he would say.

It was a good year, and the summer days were long and relaxing as the sun shone down on the well-watered crops that had sprouted beautifully under the plentiful spring rains. Now each green stalk of grain stretched upward toward the warmth of the heavens while Melkhana and Adah sat on the edge of the wagon watching the reward of their labor as it swayed in the slight breeze. Adah had drawn a bucket of fresh water for them to drink, and they sat there taking in the beauty of their life.

In the afternoons, Adah would begin working her magic over the fire with the herbs, grains, and legumes while Melkhana went to the fields to look over his crops and plan for the upcoming harvest.

Chapter 7

The Nightmare

One chilly afternoon, as the sun was beginning to go down and her well-seasoned lentils were getting cold, Adah walked to the edge of the yard and shielded her eyes from the glare of the setting sun, wondering what was keeping her husband. She could see him but couldn't make out what he was doing. He seemed to be bending over.

Maybe he had dropped one of his tools or had come upon a small, injured animal of some sort, but he wasn't getting up. Adah began to walk faster. Then she was running. Something wasn't right! "Melkhana!" she called urgently. "Melkhana, are you okay?" Adah began to feel panic wash over her. "Melkhana!"

No answer. Now she was sobbing and crying out, "Help, somebody come and help!" As she reached where Melkhana's body lay slumped over, he seemed to have been on his knees. Had his heart just stopped beating? He was not breathing, and his lips were blue. Horrible memories of the death of her brother Caleb were beginning to replay themselves in her mind.

As she touched his shoulder and pulled him up, she realized he was bleeding from the abdomen. Increased horror washed over Adah as she realized he had been stabbed. Who had…? How did…? Why would anyone want to hurt this man - this gentle, kind man who meant the world to her? Then she became irrational. She laid him back and began trying to drag him to the house. Maybe she could save him! Maybe if she just washed the wound. Maybe he would breathe again. "No, nooo!" Adah panicked. "This can't be real!"

So desperate were her efforts that Adah didn't realize she wasn't alone. Suddenly she was grabbed from behind - grabbed by rough hands and strong arms! Who was this? Had someone come to help? The voices were not familiar to her, and the language was not even Hebrew. There were at least two men, and they bound her with ropes so quickly she had no opportunity to try to free herself.

"Let me go!" Adah cried out as she struggled against them. Her voice was raspy from her efforts and the emotion of the whole terrifying scenario. "Who are you? What do you want? Help! Somebody help me!"

"Who could this be?" Adah's mind flew into action. These men had thickly accented language that seemed to be… possibly

Anatolian? Adah had heard merchants in the marketplace back home who were from the north country of Lebanon. She had also heard of bad men, men who would plunder the belongings of others. Maybe they had come to steal valuable things.

"I'll give you whatever you want from the house! Please, let me go, and I'll give you whatever you want! Just let me tend to my husband, please!" Adah's voice trailed off in a quivering plea; then she broke into desperate sobs.

The men didn't even acknowledge her pleas or cries. It was as if they had trapped a lamb and were completely unaware or unconcerned with its bleating.

When Adah realized her cries would get her nowhere, she tried to make out some of their words, but the only word she could understand and distinguish from the others was *kole.* Were these men slave traders? But then she heard them speak of Tyre and she was certain. Tyre was a port and trade city in Lebanon. There were many markets there, markets where merchants came from far away lands to buy and sell. They traded many things - food, clothing, furnishings, and yes, even slaves. Her heart went numb as fear paralyzed her whole body and mind. She was no longer able to struggle. They dragged her to their cart, threw her in the back, and headed west. She knew it was west because they rode into the sunset, toward where her father had told her was the Mediterranean Sea.

Adah lay in the bed of the rough wooden cart, still bound with ropes that hurt her wrists. Cold and sore from hours of bumping along the rugged terrain, her body was in pain, but her soul was in sheer agony at the loss of her beloved husband and in fear for herself. She knew her chances of rescue were slim as most people would never travel at this time of night and they were not likely to cross another human being until morning.

At first, she stiffened herself against the fierce bumping but then realized she was being jostled toward the rear opening of the cart; and so, with each tormenting bump, Adah desperately lunged backward. Eventually, she fell out, painfully hitting the ground with a thud. She hoped she could run away and obscure herself before the men would notice she had escaped. They were only a few hours from her home, and she probably knew this area better than they. But when she fell, the noise of the jostling wagon changed due to the absence of her weight, and one of the men turned and saw that she was gone. Adah tried to scramble to her feet and run before they could reach her, but she stumbled and fell. With her hands tied, she was unable to balance and catch herself. The men captured her with ease and administered cruel blows and harsh scoldings. They returned her to the cart, this time tying her feet together and securing them to the ropes that held her hands behind her back. They then secured her to the side of the cart. All hope of escape was gone, and she lay there defeated, hopeless, and in more pain from this awkward position.

A shiver ran through her all the way to her core. It was a two-fold shiver of cold and terror. The cool, damp night air was settling down around her. Earlier, when she had left the house to check on Melkhana, the sun had not yet set, and she hadn't planned on being out long, so she had not taken her cloak. Now, here she was on the cold, hard wood, wearing nothing more than her thin linen dress. Her arms, hands, legs, and feet were paining her from lack of proper circulation, and her back ached from being so sharply arched. These men had no human concern for her at all. If they would kill her beloved husband so cruelly, there was no telling what else they would do to her.

After a number of hours, the cart stopped, and one of the men came to the back and lay down beside her. Another cold streak of terror stabbed her as she desperately tried to push out of her mind all the possibilities this could mean, but the man covered himself with a cloak and went to sleep.

The next time she felt the cart stop, the man who had slept next to her rose and took over driving while the first driver came to lie next to her and take his rest. When she could hear from the rhythm of his breathing that he was asleep, Adah took some comfort in the warmth his body provided. Her shivering subsided somewhat, and she drifted in and out of sleep.

Hours later, they stopped again, and Adah could detect the first signs of daylight. The men covered her with a heavy blanket made of goat's hair that smelled like it had, indeed, been slept on by goats. As the sun continued rising in the sky, the blanket became uncomfortably warm, but she didn't want to find out if they would strike her again if she were to make noise or protest. When they stopped at a small village market to get food, one of the men stayed with the cart to prevent anyone from seeing her. Although she could smell the appetizing food they were eating, all they gave her was some stale water from their flask and yesterday's old, tough bread. Adah longed for some fresh water; she disliked tepid water so much.

She couldn't be certain, although she tried to keep track, but it seemed the journey had lasted for days. Then one day, they slowed the wagon and pulled it off the road behind a thicket. She could hear the crunching of twigs beneath the wooden wheels and the scraping of branches on the side of the wagon. Then both men descended and left her there.

She listened as they quietly slipped away. This was the first time they had both left her at the same time, so after awhile, she decided to call out and see if anyone was near enough to hear her cry for help. Soon, they were back, and while one man pulled away the thick blanket that covered her, the other man raised a large piece of wood and delivered a powerful blow to her head. The pain was the last thing she remembered for quite some time.

When Adah regained consciousness, she was acutely aware of a throbbing pain in her head, but she was also aware of two more women in the wagon with her. "Oh no!" Adah moaned under her breath. As bad as she felt for herself, knowing that she now had the company of other misfortunate girls like herself brought her no comfort. Had these brutal men also killed their husbands or fathers? One of them was crying quietly as the other silently trembled beyond control. How had this happened? Were they both from the same family, or had Adah been unconscious long enough for these cruel men to abduct two women from two different places? Could she have done anything to prevent this atrocity from happening to these poor girls? Adah tried to speak to one of them, but the largest man turned around and struck her with a long stick, so she resigned herself to a dreadful silence.

Counting the first frightening, agonizing night, Adah thought it was possibly near the end of the fifth night when they stopped at a place other than a random inn or spot on the side of the road. The men seemed to be greeting people who were familiar to them. Was this their home? Through the darkness, Adah could make out the skeletons of a deserted market place. As the men went into a nearby house, she could smell food but not appetizing food. It smelled of fish, garlic, and stale vinegar.

Although she had not eaten anything besides a few crumbs of stale bread for days, she was not hungry. The events of the previous days had been so horrifying! Her little dream life seemed a lifetime ago, and all she was left with now was this nightmare. During the long ride, Adah had painfully resigned herself to the idea that her life was to be one long, continuous heartache without joy and without love. She decided that whoever these men were, however cruel they may be, she would not fear them. They could never do anything more grievous to her, anything that would hurt her more, than taking her beloved Melkhana from her, so she hardened herself and embraced the bitter, numb heart that had been her companion in previous years.

Even though she was cold and sore from being tied to the side of the wagon, Adah was grateful to not be in constant motion. There were burns and opened blisters from the ropes rubbing against her wrists and ankles. She lay in a pool of her own waste, unable to do anything to remedy her situation or make herself more comfortable. As the night wore on, she fell into a fitful sleep. She dreamed terrifying nightmares of blood and of Melkhana's pale, expressionless face. She dreamed of her dear parents finding Melkhana's bloodied and motionless corpse and searching desperately for her without reward. She slept and dreamed these terrible dreams until daybreak woke her with the sounds of merchants setting up their wares in the market booths.

Chapter 8

The Nightmare Continues

Standing on the auction block was more humiliating than anything in the previous years of Adah's life! The rough men, who had abducted her and forced her to leave her dear husband's dead body lying in the field for the birds and wild animals to eat, had brought her to this far away town near the sea with fish smell in the air and noise everywhere. They brought her here to be sold as a slave! Adah despaired more than she had ever despaired in her life! As the realization swept over her that she was to be sold just a few paces away from where people sold grain, cloth, and chickens, Adah felt the full blow of repudiation. This was a whole new sort of rejection!

As much as Adah didn't want anything to do with these men, it was so insulting and degrading to realize that even *they* didn't want her. Even though it was a relief to know they didn't want her for the purposes she had feared, Adah felt so dejected and undesirable! Her heart grew more numb to protect itself from the pain. She knew the love she had shared with Melkhana was too good to be true. It *was* too much to think that life would ever turn around for her. What had she done to deserve all this? But those thoughts of self-pity only brought the sting of hot tears to her eyes, and who would want to buy a sobbing slave? She dared not ruin her chances of being sold. *Anybody* who might purchase her would be better than these savage murderers who had killed her husband and taken her captive. They were dirty and smelled of garlic, cheap wine, and sweat, and they were the last men on the face of the earth that she wanted to be with.

So, naked and ashamed, Adah bit back the tears, put a defiant tilt in her chin, and held it up as though she had some dignity. She faked the bravery that glinted from her eyes as man after man came by to consider buying her. Yes, she was strong and able to work - that was obvious from her sun-browned face, her work-worn hands, and the smooth, strong muscles under her fair skin. Even though life had been cruel to her, she was still beautiful, and several men looked her over in a disgusting way as though they were considering her for more than just labor.

Her heart screamed out in humiliation and anger. One man grabbed her by the hair, and when she opened her mouth to scream out he examined her teeth like he was considering the purchase of an animal. She wanted to spit on every one of them, to scream out for her beloved Melkhana, but she strengthened her firm resolve to be purchased and stood tall and straight.

Finally, late in the day, after the sun had burned the parts of her body that had not been accustomed to exposure, one of the men who had inspected her earlier went and spoke to her captors and paid them money. He seemed old and weathered and yet strong and fit for someone of many years. His face was worn like old leather, and Adah wondered who he was, what he was like, if she was the one he was purchasing, and if so, what he may want with her. Soon, she was untied from the post and given to the man, her arms still tied behind her back. He led her to his wagon and put her in the back without saying a word to her. He did, however, cover her nakedness with a cloak, an action for which she was grateful and one that gave her a slim glimmer of hope that there may be some kindness in this man. This wagon had a closure on the back, and Adah saw no opportunity to escape the way she had tried before, so she resigned herself to not attempt that again.

Another long journey ensued. Adah could see the sun setting over the sea to her right and tried to calculate where she was and where they were going. This journey was back in the same direction from where she had been brought just the night before, toward the south. It too was a bumpy ride that lasted way into the night, and fear gripped her like before as her mind began considering all the possibilities for which this weathered old man may have purchased her. Where was he taking her? Adah had not been paying much attention last night when they had pulled into town, and she couldn't be sure now if they were even on the same road. All she could hope for was that he would go in the same direction of her home. "Home..." Adah mused, "do I even have a home? I would certainly never shame my parents by letting them know me again, and I don't ever want to see Melkhana's beautiful little farm again."

Adah's thoughts trailed off, and many hours seemed to crawl by more slowly than the dust on the side of the road until, finally, the man pulled the wagon to a stop in front of what seemed in the darkness to be a cave.

Was this a cave dweller? Is this where he lived, or had he brought her out here in the wilderness for some evil reason? Exhausted and confused, Adah rubbed the tears and dust from her eyes onto her shoulder and struggled to sit up, hands still tied. Her neck, back, and shoulders ached from the awkward position of her hands being tied behind her for days; her hands stung with the sensation of stabbings from lack of circulation, and the painfully burned parts of her skin were reminding her of the day's humiliation.

The man came around to the back of the wagon, untied her, and gave her a drink from his canteen and an additional cloak. "You sleep here in the wagon for the rest of the night, and when morning comes I'll introduce you to my family." These were the first words he had spoken to her, and Adah was very much relieved to hear him speak in a tongue she could understand and was somewhat reassured to hear some mention of family. Then he left her alone and disappeared into the cave.

"Family?" she wondered. Adah's mind was blurry with exhaustion, so she obeyed and went to sleep in the wagon. It seemed she slept for days, and when she awoke, it was to the sound of several people. The sun was shining so brightly in her eyes, she thought maybe she had slept until noonday. Adah could hear the inquisitive voices of two women and some children who were surrounding the wagon. Adah sat up, rubbed the sleep from her eyes, and tried to focus enough to see who was inspecting her.

"My name is Miriam," the oldest woman said - she must have been in her mid-forties - "and this is Yadah, our husband's second wife. You will be his third, and we are very happy he has brought you. Please, come and we will wash you and feed you. Jaheem, will be coming to see you soon, and we want you to be well cared for."

Chapter 9

Jaheem the Bedouin

"Could this be happening?" Adah silently wondered. Did she say I'm to be his third wife? Well, that's different. And..." she smirked with cynicism, "this should be easy - one-third of the work. I never considered that my life would take this twist, and curiously, I'm sort of okay with it. Considering the alternatives, maybe it won't be so bad..." Adah's thoughts were interrupted as Miriam came behind the curtain to bring more hot water from the fire.

So there was a feast and a ceremony, and Adah became the third and youngest wife of Jaheem, the Bedouin goat farmer who was as wealthy as a sheik, and yet he moved wherever his herds could feed. He and his family lived in tents or well-cleaned caves. Sometimes Jaheem would go away for a week or more, but he always came back to his wives and children, and they always killed a goat and feasted when he returned. They were a happy little clan.

Adah was fairly happy too with Jaheem, Miriam, and Yadah. She learned many new ways of cooking with what nature had to offer in this barren landscape they called home. She also taught Miriam and Yadah some of her favorite recipes and gardening tips. She learned to understand and communicate in their Bedouin dialect and grew to appreciate many of their customs.

Most of all, Adah grew to love Miriam and Yadah's children and looked forward to the day when she would have her own. Jaheem came in to her often, yet she did not conceive.

After time went on and she still had not conceived, Jaheem became more and more forceful with her until again the experience became painful for her. He never yelled at her or hit her, but when she had been his wife for two years without conception, Jaheem put her back into the wagon without saying a word and began the trip back north... or was it east? At this point, Adah could not really be sure where she had been living the last two years and neither could she be sure where Jaheem was taking her. In a way, it didn't even seem to matter.

The pain in Adah's heart began again to grow slowly, the way water gradually but eventually boils, as she realized she was leaving her new, odd, little family, never to return again. Jaheem had not even given her the opportunity to say goodbye. The lump in her throat grew until she thought she would not be able to swallow or even breathe. If only she had a drink of water... Without saying a word to Jaheem, she lay down on the floor of the wagon and allowed a river of silent tears to flow until the wooden planks of the wagon were soaked and muddy.

Why was she never the one to be cherished? Why couldn't she bare a child? She had conceived once before. What had gone wrong? Why couldn't she conceive again? Why had God turned His back on her? God... did she even believe in God anymore? She decided that it hurt too much to hope. She had hoped for happiness with Hassan, and he had rejected her. She had hoped to be redeemed by Zephniah, but he had disdained her and rejected her too. She had *really* hoped for happiness with Melkhana and actually found it, but that had been ripped away from her. Finally, she had allowed herself to hope again with Jaheem.

Jaheem had not been unkind to her, but it was evident that he was rejecting her too. He was obviously not kind or he would not be taking her back to the auction. Adah added Jaheem to her list of those she hated. She felt stronger when she hated people, so she decided to embrace her hatred. She hated them all! She hated her father for changing, she hated Hassan for hurting her, she hated Zephniah for scorning her, she even hated Melkhana for dying. She hated Jaheem for giving up on her, and she hated God for allowing her to still be alive. Then the tears stopped and she sat up. That was it! She would choose not to hurt anymore - she would just hate. She leaned against the side of the wagon, glowered for a while at the hot, dusty road as it disappeared into the distance behind her, and eventually drifted off to sleep. They traveled for two days, and then the trip was over.

But it was not to the auction that Jaheem took her. Adah was confused to awaken to the noises of a small village rather than a busy, fishy port town. She sat up and looked around. In front of them was an inn, a stable to the left, and a row of houses to the right along the narrow road. Just before the road disappeared around the bend there was a small well. While Adah was looking around, taking in the landscape of this curious little village, Jaheem went into the inn and came back out in about fifteen minutes.

"You are going to live here now," he told her. "Adah, you are beautiful; you've been a very lovely wife, and I have enjoyed you. Now I give you to this man who is in need of a strong woman to keep the inn. He doesn't need you to bear any children, but he needs a woman who can clean and cook, and you can do both very well!"

Jaheem kissed Adah on the forehead then bowed down low before her, turned to climb onto the front of the wagon, made a clicking sound to his mule, and drove away. When he was out of sight, Adah turned to look around. After she had taken in her surroundings for a few minutes, she walked to the door and entered the inn.

Chapter 10

Simon the Inn Keeper

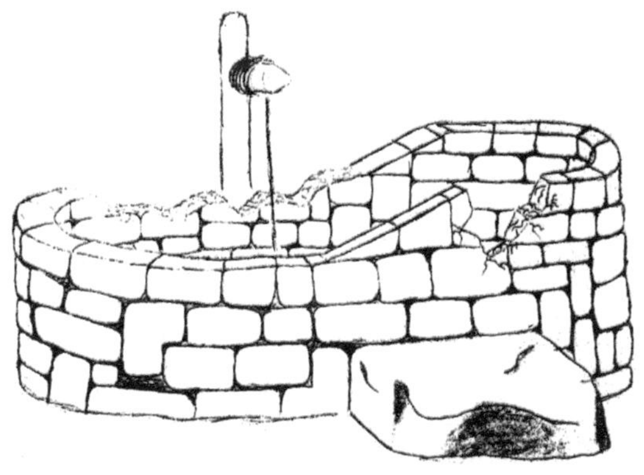

Simon was in his fifties and had a wife, Silome, who was around twenty-two years old. Silome had eight children under the age of twelve and was expecting the ninth. "This must be why Simon needs a working girl," Adah thought.

The very next day, Simon took Adah to the gate of the village to have an official marriage performed. Then they returned to the inn, and Adah settled in with her new family. She walked in the door, took the heavy bucket of water out of Silome's hand, and began washing the floors of the inn. To Adah there was something eerie about seeing a pregnant woman with a heavy water bucket in her hand, and she told Silome that she was not to carry anything heavy until after the baby came. Silome looked curiously at her but gratefully turned, picked up her one-year-old, and started tending to the needs of the small child.

Adah was accustomed to work and found comfort in it. When she cleaned a room at the inn it sparkled, and soon her cooking was talked about all around the village. Within a few short months, Adah had finally found an identity for herself that didn't include someone loving her. She denied that the thirst for acceptance and affection consumed her on the inside. She commanded her heart to learn to be happy with the dignity of her work. She decided she did not need love and that she would never seek it again.

Although Simon showed eruptive flares of temper from time to time, Adah learned how to avoid irritating him and resigned herself to making a decent life here in the shadow of the inn's kitchen.

Two years went by and Adah stopped nursing her seething hatred every night as she lay down to sleep alone. Her mind would race ahead to the following day and the meals she would plan. Simon began allowing her to hire out as a cook to the wealthy people of the village when they were having a celebration, and the name *Adah* became known as synonymous with good food and excellent hospitality.

Younger men would sometimes ask Simon why he was wasting the youth of such a beautiful, young woman behind a scrubbing brush and over the cooking fire, but Simon was so taken with his fertile young Silome that he never seemed to give Adah any other consideration beyond her fine working abilities, something for which Adah told herself she was grateful.

But Silome died during the birth of her tenth baby, and after a time of severe grieving Simon grew more demanding of Adah. Now, she was expected to take care of the inn, the kitchen, *and* the children while Simon was out in the village all day every day. What was more, he eventually began coming in her room at night and was evidently trying to impregnate her. And so Adah's recurring nightmare began all over again.

Adah decided not to wait to see what would happen. Simon had not had an angry outburst for some time now. Maybe the grief of losing Silome had mellowed him. "I'm older now and much more experienced with men than I used to be." With this thought, she began to formulate a plan in her mind. She remembered those long talks she had with Melkhana and was hopeful she could approach Simon in such a way as to make him feel she saw him as a mature man, able and willing to hear her out. Maybe if she could convince him that she saw him as a caring man, he would actually see himself that way and listen to her patiently.

Adah prepared Simon's favorite meals for a whole week. She smiled often and behaved herself in the most adoring way she knew how. Simon seemed to enjoy it. He glanced her way often and demonstrated his ravishing love on her at night.

Then one morning she woke Simon by gently rubbing his chest. Propped on one elbow beside him, she arranged her hair slightly, put on what past experiences had proven to be her most successful smile, and asked if she could talk to him about something.

Curious, Simon urged her on, "What is it, my dove? What is on your mind?"

Adah told him how happy she was to keep his inn and how much she appreciated the opportunities he gave her to serve as hostess at other celebrations. She complimented his children and his fathering skills. "But," she continued, "perhaps, if you can afford it, you may want to consider getting another wife if you want to have more children." It was painful for her, but she told him she had not been very successful in the past in her attempts to bear children.

Simon lifted himself up over Adah. "What do you mean, Girl? Are you telling me that you are barren and have never told me?" he shouted.

Adah tried to remain composed and not let Simon know she was rattled by his outburst. "I was pregnant once before. I know I *can* conceive, but I lost the baby. It was the saddest, most..."

"You LOST A BABY!" Simon yelled, "Like you lost Silome and my tenth child?" Now Simon was completely irrational and erupting with hot fury. "After all this time, you tell me you can't bring a child into this world? What kind of woman are you? How long did you plan to deceive me? Did you conspire with that swindler Jaheem to help him take my money through trickery and dishonesty?"

"I never told you anything. I thought you understood that I was only to be a work girl. I thought Jaheem told you, I..."

"You have beguiled me, you, you..." he sputtered. "You think you can defraud me and get away with it?" Simon's voice was shrill with rage, and his stale morning breath was repugnant as his spittle showered her face.

At this, Simon shoved her off the bed. She tried to stand, but he grabbed her by the throat and pushed her up against the wall. He struck her repeatedly until her face was bloody and bruised.

Adah's mind was awhirl. This news that had set him off was painful enough for her without the beating! He was indeed a cruel and unreasonable man! She wanted to get away and hated Simon more and more with each agonizing blow!

When he was satisfied that she had been sufficiently punished, Simon threw her to the floor, kicked her once to finish the job, and walked out.

As soon as Adah was able, she tried to pick herself up. She heaved herself to her hands and knees at first and realized she was bleeding profusely from her mouth and nose. She went to the water bucket to clean up before any of the children awoke from the noise and came to see what the commotion was all about. While she was washing and trying to stop the bleeding, Simon came back in and rebuked her for getting blood on the floor.

"This is an inn! Don't you know I'm expected to host guests here? Get your mess cleaned up before anyone comes!"

"I'll just go get more water," Adah said flatly as she took the water bucket and left.

She half-walked, half-staggered to the well, set the bucket down on the ground, and, without knowing where to go, kept walking. "Where am I going?" Adah thought. "Nobody here is going to help me. They'll send me back to Simon. He is my husband, after all, and I have no right to walk away. But I don't care what they do to me; I'm not going back voluntarily. They can stone me if they choose. Then, at least, my miserable life will all be over."

Since Adah had decided she was never going back, she just kept walking. She walked to the edge of the village and continued on past the last few houses and on into the wilderness.

Adah walked until she fell down. As she lay there, she rested until she gained enough strength to walk on. Then she heaved herself up and stumbled on. All through the day she followed this pattern of walking, falling, and resting, then walking some more.

The sun began to set to her right so she knew she was walking south but to where she did not know. When Jaheem had brought her to Simon's village, she had been so turned around that she was not sure of any direction. She hoped she was not on the path that would take her back to that dreadful port city where she had been auctioned. All she could see before her was wilderness and a dusty path that wound here and there over the hills in front of her.

She knew it was dangerous to travel at night. Groups of men didn't even travel after the setting of sun, but what could anyone do to her that had not already been done? "What, will they hurt me? Will they rape me? Will they sell me? Maybe they will take me to a far away land, tie me to the top of an altar on a hill, and burn my body as a sacrifice to a false god," she mused, numbly sarcastic. Adah knew she was probably being more dramatic than the situation called for. Why was she thinking like this? But her mind was too overwhelmed with grief and fury at the injustice of it all, and she couldn't help herself. How bad could it be if robbers were to capture her? She had nothing for them to take, nothing except her very life, and she was at the point where she would be willing to give that away.

Adah stopped and rested again for about an hour and then got up to go on farther. If someone came looking for her from Simon's village, she wanted to be far enough away that they wouldn't find her. Where was she going? Adah did not know, but she kept walking into the night. At some point, she collapsed from the weariness and crawled over beside a rock, sucked the fluid out of a shrubby plant growing nearby in a feeble attempt to soothe her terrible thirst, then curled up and shivered until morning.

There was some comfort to feel the sun on her throbbing face as she awoke the next morning, but when she tried to open her eyes, only one would open. She reached her hand up and gingerly felt her face. The swelling from yesterday's beating was quite extensive, and when she grimaced, it pained her terribly. Not only was her eye swollen shut but her lip was swollen too, and that's when she began to feel the inside of her lip with her tongue and realized three of her teeth were missing. Simon had beaten her so severely! He had taken one of the only things the other men had left behind, her beauty. She lay there, still moist from the morning dew, sore and aching, and Adah cried until there was no more heart left in her.

Where was she? Where were her parents? Were they even still alive somewhere? How many years had it been since she had seen them? Did they even still live on the small little farm with the rolling hills and the stream nearby? How had she come to this place in her life where no one cared? When the murderers of Melkhana had taken her, had her father searched for her, or had he merely dismissed the troubled thought of her very existence and gone on with his weary life? Why, when Adah found herself in such a desperate place, would she think of her father? Why couldn't she dismiss the thought of him the way he had probably dismissed her?

Thirst began to engulf her, and Adah got up and wandered on down the road, eating little bits from juniper bushes here and there. Late in the afternoon, two days later, she saw a group of travelers in the distance. Quickly, like a scared animal, Adah scurried off the path and hid herself in the brush behind some rocks. She didn't want anyone to see her. As they passed, she entertained the thought to follow them from a distance and sneak in to take their food and water when they stopped for the night. Adah watched the canteens wobble on the straps around their shoulders as they walked by. She mindlessly licked her dry and cracked lips. She had suffered quite a bit in her life, but she had never been this hungry, thirsty, and desperate before.

As she thought it through, Adah decided they couldn't have been walking too far since the small children traveling with them were so lively and cheerful. Surely there was a village nearby somewhere. So, abandoning her original plans to follow them, she continued on in the direction from which the travelers had come.

Chapter 11

Sychar

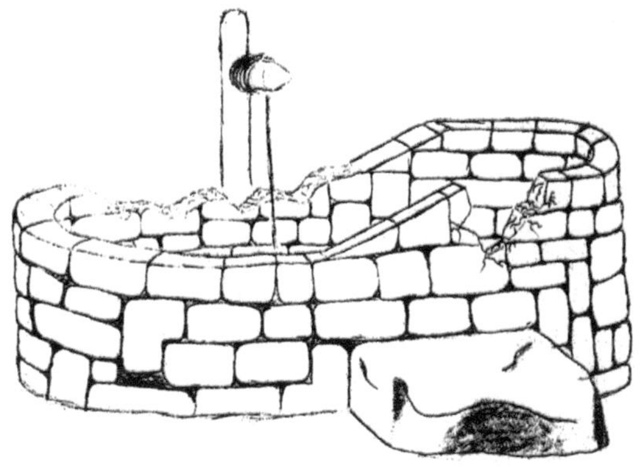

It was dusk when Adah stumbled into a small town after all the villagers had gathered in their homes. She found a well there at the edge of the village and lay down beside it to wait for morning. Surely someone would come with a bucket when the sun came up, and maybe she could beg a drink of water from them. The sparse fluid she had been able to suck from the juniper berries had not been enough, and she desperately needed water! Food, too, but most of all water.

Adah's face and eye throbbed and oozed from infection that had set in over the past few days. Her whole body ached from the beating, fever, the harsh conditions of sleeping on stony, damp ground, and exposure to the night elements. Bug bites covered her legs and arms, and her hair was tangled and matted with debris from sleeping on the ground. She was dirty and smelled terrible. At this point, however, she didn't care how horrifying her appearance must have been. She was in survival mode and none of that mattered anymore. So she huddled against the rock wall surrounding the well and waited.

As she slept and woke throughout the night Adah thought something felt strangely familiar about this well. Or was she just beginning to hallucinate? Adah peered into the darkness and tried to figure out why the path that led from the well into the village seemed so much like she had been here before. She could almost make out a few houses nearest the well, but through the darkness, with only one weary eye open and the blurry fog that clouded her mind, she just could not place when or if she had ever passed this way before.

The next morning, when she awoke, the young girls and women had gathered to draw water for their morning chores, but they had all stopped a distance back from Adah, huddling together and wondering among themselves who or what this was and why it was here at their well.

Neglecting all social constraints, Adah lunged toward them. "Water, please, may I have some water," she half-mumbled, half-wheezed. These were the first words she had uttered audibly since the day of her beating, and Adah almost didn't recognize her own voice through the thick swelling in her mouth, the missing teeth, and the hoarse raspy sounds in her throat caused from dehydration.

The girls and women all shrank back in fear of this horrifying looking creature. The youngest girls ran to tell their daddies, and soon a large crowd surrounded her. Some were merciful enough to give her water. Others tried to wash her wounds to see how extensive they were. Still others demanded that she tell them who she was, to whom she belonged, and from where she had come.

Adah was too weak to answer their questions, but some of the crowd of onlookers, being half Jew, had been taught to be kind to strangers, so they took this strange woman in and cared for her. "We'll care for her until she is well enough to be on her way," they told one another.

By the third day in the care of these kind villagers, Adah learned she was in a place called Sychar of Samaria. Sychar? Could it really be? But Adah didn't recognize any of these people, and they certainly didn't recognize her! Were these really the same people who had known her growing up and had turned away from her when Hassan ben Ruben rejected her? Were they really the ones who had refused to extend credit to her father when he had fallen on hard times? Maybe *they* were the ones to blame for her terrible life! What would her life have been if her father hadn't been so desperate for money and would have chosen a husband for her with her best interest in mind instead of trying to find someone who could pay the highest bride price? Must she really lie here and allow them to care for her and help her heal? Why should she live? So she would have to show some sort of gratitude to these savage people? Sure, they could show kindness to a wounded stranger, but she had been one of their own, and they had cast her out when reproach had befallen her! She wanted to reject every one of them the way they had rejected her! Maybe she should reveal herself to them. Then they would cast her out of the village for the miserable failure that she really was. She could go and lie in the wilderness until she died. Now she had a whole new group of people to add to the list of those she hated. Adah drifted off into a fevered sleep as she contemplated her incredible misfortune.

"There, there, my dear, you're getting better, and you will heal. You'll see," crooned the kind voice of a wrinkled old woman as she bent over Adah to gently wash her eye and lip once again with a cloth dipped in mild vinegar and mint water. Adah tried not to wince as she thought, "She's right; they seem to be decent enough people." They were, in fact, her blood relatives, her people. This *was* the village of her birth. Things seemed better this morning, so Adah decided to stay there until she became strong enough to move on. If she didn't tell them, no one would ever know she was the same Adah they had known years earlier. There was nothing left for them to recognize. Her gentle nature had long since been replaced by hatred and bitterness and where she once had beauty, she was left with scars and the hardened face and rigid jaw of resentment.

Adah worked for whomever would give her food, but she still had hatred in her heart for everyone and refused to make any close friends. Around town she occasionally recognized an old friend, and they would peer curiously at her as if they had known someone like her in another life and in another place, but they could never place her. She was a strange, elusive woman, and they just could not figure her out - nor did they particularly want to.

The disfigurement of her face made them cringe inside and avoid her altogether, and Adah was comfortable with being left alone.

At one point, Adah was hired to do some gardening for a wealthy young lady about her age and was mindlessly humming to herself as she worked. She had been working for some time when she felt the presence of someone watching her and looked up to find herself face to face with Hassan ben Ruben. He had aged some but was still strikingly handsome with a bit of distinguishing gray at his temples. He had been watching her, head tilted slightly, trying unsuccessfully to remember where he had seen her before.

Pulling herself from the past, Adah's mind flew into action. She didn't want him to recognize her! She stopped humming immediately, tightened the back of her throat to disguise her voice, and spoke harshly and disrespectfully to him. He fired her at once and chased her away like a stray animal, and she was grateful.

One day, Adah overheard some ladies in the market discussing how Harmon and Dina had come back to live out their last days with Adin, their eldest son. Her heart grew hard as the hatred smoldered and almost burst into flames of outrage right there in public. She turned her head to the side, closed her eyes tightly, and swallowed hard to keep her lips from curving into a twisted expression of disgust. Deep down inside, she knew she should go to them and let them know she was alive. She knew she owed them that, but all the years of justifying her resentment had distorted her thinking, and she didn't even feel tenderness toward her mother, much less her father.

Chapter 12

Benedab

As time went on, Adah took up with a dejected sort of fellow named Benedab. She knew he was a rough character and not very honorable, but she felt lower and more reproachable in the wholesome company of the families who had helped her. "At least with Benedab," Adah thought to herself, "I have as much dignity as he does."

Adah had been sleeping in different places. She didn't want to stay with anyone long enough to really feel like she owed them much, so she would move around. She continued to eat in Benedab's house though, and one evening he asked her to stay. She did, and they became close - too close. It wasn't right, Adah knew, but he was all she had, so she justified herself. It felt as if he understood her and she understood him. Life had been cruel to them both.

The only problem was that Benedab had these strange episodes where he would erupt with irrational absurdities, gibberish, rantings, and madness every once in a while. Some said he was possessed by a devil that took him over on occasion. Others said he was a fool and not right in his mind, but Adah knew his mind was right most of the time. He just had this problem ever so often.

When Benedab erupted, he would yell and scream obscenities and throw things around. If anyone were near, he would hurt them. No one seemed to be able to soothe or calm him during these times, and he seemed to have super-human strength. Most people stayed clear of him, but Adah felt sorry for him and would just hide when he had one of his spells. "They *are* scary, but nothing could be worse than all the other things I've been through," she told herself. "At least he can't reject me as a wife since we are not married." Adah thought it through. If he ever started to seem displeased with her, she would just leave before he could throw her out. Adah decided this would be her best course of action - reject him before he could reject her.

The longer she lived with Benedab, the more people of the village continued to avoid her too. She was grateful to the ones who had helped her, but they were suspicious of her because she had never told them where she had come from. Now they had reason to scorn her because she was obviously playing the harlot with Benedab. He had never gone to the gates to conduct a proper marriage, and Adah was now carrying his child.

So Adah made it her habit to go to the well at noontime when the sun was hot and the other ladies were busy making a mid-day meal for their families. This way she didn't have to answer questions or deal with the way people would sneak a peek at the scars on her face and wonder what happened to the rest of her teeth.

Adah knew she wasn't worth much. The bitterness this realization brought when she thought about it caused her not to think about it too often. She would just go on, existing in this hopeless, colorless life of reproach and shame.

Hopefully some day, she would be able to rear a child well enough that he would become someone important. Then she would be able to feel that she had accomplished something worthwhile before she died. "And," she mused morbidly, "the sooner I die, the better."

Gone were the dreams of rearing a happy family the way her mother had. They seemed unrealistic under these circumstances. Gone was the hope that she would ever walk with dignity into the marketplace or hold her head up as she passed others in the street. Adah had resolved herself to a life of dreary survival. She longed to be excited about this child that grew in her womb and ached to feel the joy and anticipation of motherhood every time she felt the baby move within her, but the shame and reproach of being a harlot weighed heavily upon her conscience, and she afforded herself no such privilege.

It was on that day - the day she thought those depressing thoughts - that she came wearily to the well...

Chapter 13

Jesus

He left Judaea, and departed again into Galilee. And he must needs go through Samaria. Then cometh he to a city of Samaria, which is called Sychar, near to the parcel of ground that Jacob gave to his son, Joseph. Now Jacob's well was there. Jesus therefore, being wearied with his journey, sat thus on the well: and it was about the sixth hour. There cometh a woman of Samaria to draw water: Jesus saith unto her, Give me to drink. (For his disciples were gone away unto the city to buy meat.) Then saith the woman of Samaria unto him, How is it that thou, being a Jew, askest drink of me, which am a

> *woman of Samaria? For the Jews have no dealings with the Samaritans. Jesus answered and said unto her, If thou knewest the gift of God, and who it is that saith to thee, Give me to drink; thou wouldest have asked of him, and he would have given thee living water. The woman saith unto him, Sir, thou hast nothing to draw with, and the well is deep: from whence hast thou that living water? Art thou greater than our father Jacob, which gave us the well, and drank thereof himself, and his children, and his cattle?* (John 4:3-12).

Adah remembered the lessons her father had taught her about their history. This *was* the well their ancestor Jacob had digged and it *was* deep. And who was this man talking to her? No one besides Benedab had spoken to her willingly in over a year, but this man didn't even seem disgusted by her. There was something intriguing about his gentle way. He seemed respectable, and no self-respecting person would normally have anything to do with someone of her station. But he also seemed respectful toward her as if he thought she had something of value worth respecting. Adah found this curious because even her own villagers would not talk with her anymore. Yet he, although a Jew, spoke of the things of God with someone as lowly as she. He was different from anyone she had ever encountered. Was he...? could he be...? And this water he spoke of... Adah had been thirsty for as long as she could remember. Her mouth was dry, her heart was dry, and even her hands were dry and cracked. What did he mean when he said he could give her "living water"?

The man motioned toward the water in the well.

> *Jesus answered and said unto her, Whosoever drinketh of this water shall thirst again: But whosoever drinketh of the water that I shall give him shall never thirst; but the water that I shall give him shall be in him a well of water springing up into everlasting life* (John 4:13-14).

Now Adah couldn't help herself. She didn't know who he was. Well, she had an idea, but... well… she didn't know *for sure* who he was. She didn't know what this strange feeling was about. It was almost like... like hope! Yes, it was hope that she was feeling. Adah had promised herself long ago not to ever be foolish enough to hope again, but this was so different! This man didn't want from her the things other men had wanted. He was offering her something different. He was offering something real, something eternal!

Adah continued to question. Could this man she had just met possibly be the same as the Jehovah her father had taught her about? Had the Yahweh of old appeared unto her? What could it hurt to take him at his word and try his water?

> *The woman saith unto him, Sir, give me this water, that I thirst not, neither come hither to draw. Jesus saith unto her, Go, call thy husband, and come hither* (John 4:15-16).

Adah froze. Wait, why did he want her to call her husband? Was this some sort of legal agreement he was intending for her to enter into in order to get this water? A woman wasn't qualified to conduct legal business. This *had* to be why he was asking for her husband. Immediately, Adah felt defensive.

> *The woman answered and said, I have no husband. Jesus said unto her, Thou hast well said, I have no husband: For thou hast had five husbands; and he whom thou now hast is not thy husband: in that saidst thou truly* (John 4:17-18).

Now Adah was completely stupefied. What kind of man *was* this? The people of her own village didn't even know who she was, but this gentle man seemed to look into her very soul, past all the ugliness that would repel the most hardened of men, and see the truth of her painful life. He seemed to know everything about her, and yet he didn't hesitate to have dealings with her. He did not reject her. Her mind was full of wonder!

He *was* a man - that was certain. She had seen him drink the water she drew for him. And yet, He seemed like God! Adah felt bewildered. Could the one true God who created everything have possibly become a man, appeared to her, and told her all these things? Adah pondered some of the things He had said...

She realized that life eternal came from knowing that this man, Jesus, was the only true God (John 17:3).

As she pondered, Adah's mind went back to when her father used to quote his favorite prophet, Jeremiah.

> *The LORD hath appeared of old unto me, saying, Yea, I have loved thee with an everlasting love: therefore with loving kindness have I drawn thee* (Jeremiah 31:3).

It seemed like it was yesterday, and she could hear her father's voice quoting the words even now. It was a prophecy of promise from Jehovah to His people. Adah thought about how God was promising to give the people of Israel a new and prosperous life. She used to imagine those Israelites and their desolate lives, having strayed from their God, and how beautiful it must have been to return to Him and let Him restore the life they had always wanted. Now, it was like she was living in that dream. God had come to her. He was offering her a new life. He was offering her everlasting love. It seemed like He was drawing her with His loving kindness even now!

Adah felt an overwhelming urge to proclaim this man to be God, but she still felt some hesitation. Maybe He was just a man who was sent from God and not God Himself... Adah cautiously decided to say her thoughts aloud and see if this dream would evaporate.

> *The woman saith unto him, Sir, I perceive that thou art a prophet* (John 4:19).

The words had been spoken and nothing happened. He was still there before her. "What now?" she wondered. Adah had hoped for a better life and a new start so many times and been disappointed. She was having a bit of trouble being certain that she could trust this man.

"I'll challenge him, that's what I'll do," she thought. "He seems to know all about me as if he were indeed sent from God. And he seems to be genuinely caring. But if I challenge him, then we'll see how gentle he really is."

> *Our fathers worshipped in this mountain; and ye say, that in Jerusalem is the place where men ought to worship. Jesus saith unto her, Woman, believe me, the hour cometh, when ye shall neither in this mountain, nor yet at Jerusalem, worship the Father. Ye worship ye know not what: we know what we worship: for salvation is of the Jews. But the hour cometh and now is, when the true worshippers shall worship the Father in spirit and in truth: for the Father seeketh such to worship him. God is a Spirit: and they that worship him must worship him in spirit and in truth. The woman saith unto him, I know that Messias cometh, which is called Christ: when he is come he will tell us all things. Jesus saith unto her, I that speak unto thee am he* (John 4:20-26).

Adah's breath caught in her throat. So it WAS true! The M-M-M...the Messiah had really come! Why had He come to her? How could she find her father? She had to let him know! He *had* been right! She had to spread the news!

> *The woman then left her waterpot, and went her way into the city, and saith to the men, Come, see a man, which told me all things that ever I did: is not this the Christ? Then they went out of the city, and came unto him* (John 4:28-30).

She wanted to boldly proclaim to everyone in the village that, "This IS the Christ, this IS God!" But she knew she had no status of credibility among the people. She was so uncertain about her own identity. What if they would not believe her? She decided to frame her statement as a question for their consideration, "Is not this the Christ?" It had worked! They had gone to see Jesus for themselves! This made Adah so happy to have been able to share this great news!

As she walked on, Adah knew this man, the Messiah, could heal her of all her brokenness. This meant that none of her failures were so terrible that she couldn't find hope again! Nothing seemed hopeless in light of the power and love of this man she had just met! She knew He could heal Benedab of the torment he endured. Even if it *was* because of a devil, Adah had a strong confidence that the Messiah could deliver him. She had grown to love Benedab in her own way. He was a crippled soul, but she was too, and now there was hope for both of them!

Adah was so sure she had found the Messiah! She felt a lifting of such heaviness when she recognized that the man she had just met was God, the almighty Jehovah and Creator of everything.

But there was more to Jesus than hope and a promise of help. There was a holiness, a righteousness that Adah realized she wasn't qualified to receive. She recognized that she was going to need more from Jesus than merely a freedom from her past. She was not going to be able to sustain this difference inside of her unless she received more from Him. She needed more than a feeling of hope, more than reassurance. She needed to be changed, changed on the inside, and Jesus was the only One who was going to be able to make the change in her.

Adah recognized that there was a sovereignty about Jesus, a demand for more than allegiance or loyalty. His sovereignty demanded that she abandon all her other views of who God is.

She had thought of Him as the One who should make her happy and heal her family. She had thought Him to be the One who was supposed to listen to her prayers and perform her requests. When that hadn't happened, she became disillusioned with Him. She had decided she could do better on her own because her prayers hadn't moved God the way she thought they were supposed to move Him. In fact, Adah remembered the day in the barn among the piles of grain when she had come to the conclusion that she would not trust Jehovah any longer. She had even been bitter toward Him.

Now, she realized that she had known *who* He was but she had not really *known* Him. She had thought him to be a God who could be swayed by her desires and demands. She had altogether missed the understanding of His immutability because she thought she could change Him. She had missed the concept of His omnipresence because she thought He had not been with her at times.

Suddenly, Adah was filled with a determination to do everything within her power to receive this water Jesus was talking about. Although she was fully aware by now that she couldn't do it on her own, she was determined to do what she could. Maybe it was more than just water. Maybe it was a spiritual water that would wash and cleanse away all the ugliness inside her. If this is what it was, if it could make her truly changed, she wanted it.

She knew she had been desperately in need of help from a power far beyond her own. She knew she had come in contact with that power. She recognized that He was the only One who could change her, the only One who could save her. But that led her to the realization that she could not selfishly grab this wonderful feeling of freedom and run away with it. There was a grave awareness that fell over her. It was the awareness that she needed to know more about Jesus.

So she ran back to the well. "Jesus," Adah called breathlessly, "Master, if you would, may I ask you a few questions?"

Jesus and Adah sat for quite some time while He told her many truths she had never heard before.

"If you want to find rest for your mind, rest for your will, and rest for your emotions, then you must learn of me," He told her. "For I am meek and lowly in heart (Matthew 11:29).

"If you need to find out who you are, you must learn of me," He went on, "For at the beginning of time, I created male and female in my own image (Genesis 1:27). When you study me, you will find all things that pertain unto life and godliness, for it's through the knowledge of me that these things come (2 Peter 1:3).

"Did you know that you can escape the corruption all around you that comes from everyone having such strong desires and that you can become a partaker of the divine nature? Well, you can, but only if you receive the exceeding great and precious promises that come by the knowledge of me. For I have called you to glory and virtue (2 Peter 4:3).

"You can trust your psyche to me and me alone, for no one else really understands it. Even the prophet Jeremiah said, 'The heart is deceitful above all things and desperately...'"

"Desperately wicked: who can know it!" interrupted Adah. "I know that from the readings my father used to teach us!" (Jeremiah 17:9).

"You're right," said Jesus. "So remember to not convince yourself that you know your own motives. Your heart will trick you every time. Checking your motives is something you're always going to need my help with. Just ask, and I'll show you when there's something in your heart that is evil. For the imagination of man's heart is evil from his youth (Genesis 8:21).

"But you don't need to be afraid if you study my Word, for my Word is alive! It is very powerful and effective; it is very sharp. It's like a sword with two edges that can pierce down deep, even deep enough to distinguish between the soul and spirit. No man can tell you where your soul stops and your spirit starts. Where do the two come together? Remember, my daughter, no one will ever really understand this deep inner part of you but me. I made you, and only I truly understand how to heal this part of you. It is my Word that will discern your thoughts and the intents of your heart (Hebrews 4:12).

"This brings us to the next step that you need to be aware of, my daughter," Jesus continued. "We need to address the issue of your motives. You have received the revelation that I AM. I AM the one who created all that you see and the deep mysteries that you cannot see. I AM the one who sent Moses to speak unto Pharaoh. I AM Jehovah who provided a way in the wilderness for my people. And I AM come to you to make you one of my own. You know that now.

"When you recognized that I was God, you admitted to yourself that the only solution to your life was me. Then you responded by wanting and seeking to know more of me. I commend you for all these steps, but you must now repent of your sin. You must allow me to give you the gift of repentance that will enable you to abandon your selfish motives. For I know that you have despaired even of life itself because your life was not the way you wanted it, but you must be willing to give up your life for my sake. You must be willing to give up all the hopes and dreams of the life you would choose and be willing to live whatever life I choose for you" (Matthew 10:39, 16:24-25, Mark 8:34-35, Luke 9:23-24, 14:6-27, 17:33, John 12:25).

Adah's head was down, and she stared and picked at her rugged fingernails as she listened. "I do want to live the life You choose for me, Jesus. I'm just going to need some time to work through some things. See, my father and I used to..."

"I know all about your father, Adah," Jesus interrupted. "And that is what I mean by 'give up your life for my sake.' Year after year, you've carried around the hurt you received from your father. You've carried around the hurts you've received at the hands of other people, and you've chosen to carry around bitterness over your life not turning out the way you would have wanted it. You felt you had a right to live a happy and fulfilling life. You had the right to be cared about and protected by your father. You had the right to be cherished and understood by Hassan ben Ruben. You had the right to have been redeemed by Zephniah. There were many other times in your life that you felt your rights were violated. Well, I'm asking you to turn over all your rights to me. Give up your rights to me right now. No one will ever be able to violate your rights again because you will have none left. I want to be the one who chooses your rights. Can you trust me to choose what is best for you?"

"I do," Adah replied, "I give You my rights. That means I no longer have a grudge against my father. I have nothing to blame him for. The rights he trampled are not there anymore, and I have no offense against him." She looked up into Jesus' eyes with tears brimming in her own. "You have just asked me to do the hardest thing I've ever done - to give up my rights - but in doing that, I've just received the greatest liberty I could ever imagine!"

"This will be an ongoing process for you, Adah. Forgiveness is something you will need to do on a continual basis for the rest of your life. Do not be weary in well doing. Be prepared - you will be called on to forgive time and time again.

"You have the privilege of asking me to forgive your debts *as*, or in the same manner as, you forgive your debtors (Matthew 6:12).

"If you forgive others when they do you wrong, you will receive forgiveness from me. But if you do not forgive others, then you will not be able to receive the forgiveness that I have for you (Matthew 6:14-15).

"Be generous when you forgive. For with the same measure you distribute forgiveness, it will be with that same measure you will be able to receive forgiveness" (Luke 6:38).

As Jesus taught, there was a tender healing that was taking place in the spirit of a broken woman that day at the well. True repentance and a complete, God-given transformation of motives led directly to the remission of all sin in her life. Adah was free from every sin she had ever committed, but she was also free from every sin that had been committed against her. She had not forgotten them. She could clearly remember the day at the slave auction, but it did not hurt anymore. Just like a wound that had healed, the scar of the memory no longer brought her pain.

There were many more things Adah learned that day, but when she had received the gifts God wanted to give her, she was a new person. She had received the gift of revelation, God's grace. He had made himself known to her. She had abandoned her pride by acknowledging that He was her only hope. She had responded by seeking His ways and repented by abandoning her own selfish will. She had found true remission by forgiveness of others, and she had received the power that God was giving her to become a new creature.

Now Adah felt that she finally knew what love was. Not what she had always thought love to be, but *true* love. She knew Jesus was firmly committed to do good for her and nothing else. This was love, and she wanted more of it. Jesus had healed her from the deep pain of rejection and betrayal.

She wanted to learn to live this new life and continue to learn more about Him. She wanted others to know about Him too.

Chapter 14

The New Adah

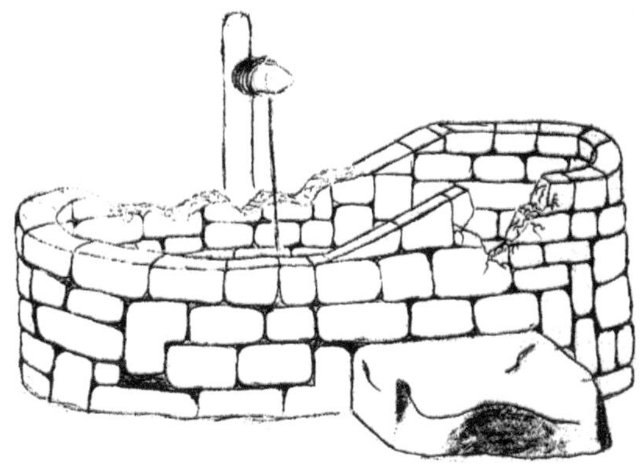

Adah was the girl who had been rejected by so many. She knew her life had sunk to the lowest levels of hatred and depravity, and if Jesus would do these things for her then He would do them for anybody! So into the village she ran, no longer concerned about hiding her true identity. Calling out to each person she passed, Adah wanted everyone to meet the Christ!

Adah passed an elderly man who walked with a bent back and a stick in his hand to steady his step. She recognized him as Hassan's father, Elder Ruben. She found herself running up to him to tell him the good news as if there had never been animosity between them. For a second Adah paused, wondering where all the hatred had gone, but she couldn't be bothered with that right now. She felt she *must* tell him. "Father Ruben, did you know the Messiah has come to make us free? It's true! He's at the well at the edge of town, even now!"

Next, Adah told some women in the marketplace who had gossiped harshly about her after the collapse of her first marriage. One of these women had also slandered Adah's father terribly. Even though Adah remembered it clearly, somehow this made no difference to her now; she just had to tell the news of Jesus.

As Adah left the marketplace, she wondered where all her resentment for these people had gone. Then she thought about all the sins of her own life. It was as though Jesus had removed their weight from her. How could she dare withhold forgiveness from anyone else?

Then she saw Ashmela, Samuel's wife and Zephniah's mother. Adah told her too, "There's a man at the edge of the city who can heal the dim vision of your tired eyes if you'll but make your way to the well where He is!"

"Adah, is that your voice I hear?" said Ashmela in a weak and trembling voice.

"Yes, it is me, but Jesus is the one you need to meet. Go now, dear Mother, and I will find you later," Adah called back as she ran on.

Adah's run slowed to a walk and she finally felt that feeling that every girl of every age wants to feel – she belonged now! Adah belonged to Jesus, He had made her His own. She could finally belong to her community! The walls of bitterness over rejection had been torn down and this was her home town!

Continuing on, telling person after person, Adah thought about the heaviness of hatred she had carried for years that was beginning to lift from her. She wondered where it had gone. Had Jesus taken it away? Or was it something He had enabled her to release and let go of by her own choice? She decided to test this new liberty she was feeling and see if it really was within her own power to attain. The real test would be to see if she could think of her father without disdain. If she could do that, then Adah knew she was really free.

So she left the center of town and set out on the road toward Adin's house. It was as if God Himself was urging her to reconcile with her family, and she was responding to whatever His bidding may be.

To her surprise, Adah felt nervous but not anxious. It was at this moment, as she walked along reflecting on the past few hours, that she realized the freedom she was feeling was indeed in direct proportion to the forgiveness she had been extending to others. This sensation of freedom obviously was a result of the forgiveness Jesus was offering to her. Adah knew she had done bad things, said bad things, thought terrible things, and she knew she needed forgiveness. Jesus had offered it to her so freely, but her ability to receive that forgiveness had been dependent upon her willingness to forgive those who had wronged her.

Could she forgive her father? Right now, Adah believed she could, but would she feel differently when she was actually standing before him? What if he was cold and indifferent toward her - could she still forgive him?

Before long she was walking up the pathway that led toward the house of her eldest brother. She hadn't been here for so many years. Should she knock on the door like a stranger? Adah decided to call out to announce her arrival the way she had done so many years ago when she was a lighthearted, happy little girl. Indeed, she felt lighthearted today!

"Helloooo! I'm here!" Adah called as she reached a bend in the road and approached the house.

Harmon, well stricken with age, stirred on his bed and rubbed his head. Was he dreaming of a time long ago? This voice he was hearing must certainly be in his imagination. No one in the family had heard news of Adah for many years. His mind briefly wandered back to the strange disappearance of his youngest daughter that happened at the same time as the brutal and mysterious murder of her husband. The sorrow of this tragedy was one he and his wife believed they would carry with them to their graves. This couldn't possibly be her! But the voice seemed so present that he found himself struggling to his feet and shuffling toward the door, if only to look out and dream some more... That voice had seemed so real!

As Harmon reached the doorway he saw Dina coming around the side of the house from the garden, her apron full of freshly picked beans. She was bent and weary, but there was a look of surprised anticipation on her face. All at once, they both saw her. From a distance, they could see a woman who looked like she could have at one time been Adah, but she seemed older and more rugged. She walked with a slight hesitation.

"Adah," Dina called out in a hope that was just barely alive, "is that you?"

At that, Adah broke into a run as she came nearer to meet her parents. As she approached, they could see the terrible scarring on her face and knew she had fallen into terrible hardships. It broke their hearts to imagine what evils had befallen her, but that didn't matter right now. All that mattered now was that their daughter was alive, she had come back, and they were together once more!

Smothered in the embrace of the trembling hands of her mother and father, Adah wept tears of joy. They were tears so pure that there was no doubt she *could* forgive her father. Then it came in another wave of that indescribable release in her spirit. Yes, Adah was experiencing the unrestrained forgiveness from God as she forgave her father. At that moment, Adah knew that even if others would continue to do her wrong, she would still be able to continue forgiving them because it was through this process that Adah received from God the forgiveness she so desperately needed. That feeling flooded over her again, that feeling of belonging! Adah was truly home!

This hope of a new life was indescribably bright and overwhelmingly joyous! Adah felt that she would hardly be able to contain the gratitude inside her heart without bursting! The only way she could imagine finding a release from all the pressure of love inside was to share it with others!

Chapter 15

God's Plan - A Deep Well?

How could something as common and non-spiritual as a deep well be a major part of God's plan? How can the common, everyday things and events in our lives be God-ordained?

When Adah left the well to go into the city, Jesus sat on the well and reflected. Because He is eternal and omniscient, He sees all time frames at the same time. He had known Adah would be here today at this well. In His divine wisdom, He had inspired His servant Jacob to dig this well some two thousand years earlier. Jacob had obeyed the plan of God and dug here, in this particular place. The Creator of every man, woman, boy, and girl saw Adah of Sychar and knew she would be rejected, betrayed, wounded, and scarred. He knew she would be in need of living water, and He made a plan to bring her to this place. He knew she would suffer thirst all her life, and He didn't prevent the pain that led to her thirst. He lovingly allowed it so that she would always crave water. He knew He could use her thirst and this well to help her be able to recognize that He was her answer.

Jesus, the Almighty God knew that Adah would be born and live in a place where Jews would not usually pass through. He knew His disciples wouldn't understand why He needed to go there, and they certainly wouldn't understand Him talking to someone of her status. He had it all planned out to send them into the city to buy food so He could minister to this wounded soul. Social constraints would require that He pass her by without speaking a word to her, but all those years before, He had a plan to reach out to her and offer healing. All those years earlier, He had urged Jacob to build this well, this meeting place, this oasis for Adah. Many had benefited from this well over the centuries, but Jesus had planned to meet Adah here and offer new life to her. Oh, how He longed for her to accept it!

Chapter 16

The Story Continues...

Just as Jesus cared for Adah, He cares for you and for me. Many years ago, before we were formed in our mothers' womb, He was setting up circumstances to bring us healing and forgiveness.

You are always going to belong to someone. You either belong to God or you belong to the carnal nature of your own flesh which is vulnerable to be owned by the enemy of your soul, the devil. The devil wants to enslave you in deep pits of bitterness and unforgiveness, but God wants you to be free! Freedom comes when you commit yourself to learning of God. You can do this by considering how His nature and His ways compare to every part of your life. Then your thinking can begin to conform to His likeness. Romans 12:2 in the New Living Translation says, "Don't copy the behavior and customs (*attitudes*) of this world, but let God transform you into a new person by changing the way you think. Then you will learn to know God's will for you, which is good and pleasing and perfect."

This transforming of your mind gives God the opportunity to reshape you into His image. Then you belong to Him, and belonging to Jesus is true freedom! When you belong to your loving Creator, you are free to become who He intended you to be. You can know true contentment because there is nothing more fulfilling than being free to live out who you were created to be!

If you've been bound by hurts that have wounded you, you *can* find freedom through forgiveness! But don't let the forgiveness process scare you. Keep your focus on learning about God, and He'll guide you through each step the way He did for Adah.

For each individual in the world, God has a plan, and it's a beautiful plan that works for anyone who will employ it.

To employ God's wonderful plan in your life, seek Him. Search the Scriptures to find who He is and what He is like. He wants you to know Him. He's yearning for you to know Him. He expects you to know Him. If you want to know Him more, read His Word. Here are some Scriptures to get you started, but these are only the beginning! You will begin to see how important it is to not just know *about* God but to really *know* Him for yourself! The following verses can bring more hope and life to you than I could ever even begin to offer you in the little story of Adah.

You can study God for the rest of your life, and there will still be more for you to learn. So get your Bible, get a note pad, and get studying. Enjoy the journey, and grow in grace!

Day 1:

Read these verses and list what God expects you to know about Him.

Hosea 13:4; 2 Thessalonians 1:7-8; Proverbs 8:35; Romans 1:16-21; 1 Corinthians 15:34; Deuteronomy 4:35; Deuteronomy 32:39; Psalm 83:18; Matthew 1:21; Exodus 15:2; Psalm 118:14,21; Isaiah 12:2; Isaiah 43:10-12; Isaiah 44:6-8; Isaiah 45:21-23; Philippians 2:10-11; Jeremiah 9:23-24; Deuteronomy 29:29; Hebrews 11:6; Matthew 10:30; Psalm 139:13

Day 2:

Read these verses and list what you learn about God's name.
Psalm 91:14-16; Isaiah 52:6; Zechariah 14:9; Acts 4:12

List what you learn about God's identity.
Exodus 15:2; Matthew 1:21; Acts 22:8; 1 John 5:20-21

Day 3:

Read these passages and mark which ones describe the following attributes of God: God is Absolute, God is Immutable, God is Omniscient, God is Sovereign, God is Omnipotent, God is Omnipresent, God is Eternal, and God is Love.

Deuteronomy 6:4; Mark 12:29; Ephesians 4:4-6; John 4:24; Acts 17:27; Psalm 139:7-13; Exodus 33:20; Colossians 1:15-16

Day 4:

Read how the Old Testament declared that the Savior (Messiah) would come and that He would be none other than God Himself. List the comparisons of those Old Testament verses to the Savior of the New Testament.

Isaiah 9:6; Malachi 2:10; Ephesians 4:6; Isaiah 7:14; Matthew 1:21-23; Isaiah 35:4-6; Luke 7:22

Day 5:

Read and list how the New Testament declares that Jesus was fully God.

Acts 20:27-28; Titus 2:13; Jude 25; 1 Corinthians 3:16-17; Ephesians 3:17; Colossians 2:8-10; Colossians 1:19

Day 6:

Read how God manifested Himself in flesh as Jesus. Why did He do this? So you and I could *know* Him! Make a list of how these verses teach who Jesus is.

1 Timothy 3:16; John 1:1,14,18; Colossians 1:15; 2 Corinthians 4:4

Day 7:

Read and list the identity that Jesus claimed.

John 10:30; John 14:6-11; John 8:19, 24, 25, 27; Exodus 15:2

Don't stop here! Ask God what He wants you to study next week...and the week after that...and the following week! Soon, you will be free!

Love God, love others, love life, and love your new freedom!

www.ingramcontent.com/pod-product-compliance
Ingram Content Group UK Ltd.
Pitfield, Milton Keynes, MK11 3LW, UK
UKHW041845190726
13854UKWH00002B/729

9 781490 840550